COOL CAREERS
WITHOUT COLLEGE
FOR PEOPLE WHO LOVE
TECH

SUSAN NICHOLS

ROSEN
PUBLISHING®

New York

Published in 2017 by The Rosen Publishing Group, Inc.
29 East 21st Street, New York, NY 10010

Copyright © 2017 by The Rosen Publishing Group, Inc.

First Edition

Library of Congress Cataloging-in-Publication Data

Names: Nichols, Susan, 1975– author.
Title: Cool careers without college for people who love tech / Susan Nichols.
Description: First edition. | New York: Rosen Publishing, 2017. | Series: Cool careers without college | Audience: Grades 7 to 12. | Includes bibliographical references and index.
Identifiers: LCCN 2016020459 | ISBN 9781508172802 (library bound)
Subjects: LCSH: Computer science—Vocational guidance—Juvenile literature. | Technology—Vocational guidance—Juvenile literature.
Classification: LCC QA76.25 .N53 2017 | DDC 004.023—dc23
LC record available at https://lccn.loc.gov/2016020459

Manufactured in China

CONTENTS

INTRODUCTION

The last thirty years will be remembered as the age of technology. What exactly is technology? In a 2013 interview with *Time* magazine's David Greelish, computer scientist Alan Kay offered this definition: "Technology is anything that wasn't around when you were born."

Let's offer a more usable definition: technology is the use of information and scientific advances in completing our work-related and personal tasks. It's applying science to enhance our routines and jobs. For example, fifty years ago, a company may have written bills to a customer by hand and mailed them via postal mail. Forty years ago, they may have typed them out. The typewriter and the word processor were forms of technology that made their work faster and easier. Now that same company may have an automated, online payment system that emails bills to clients and allows the clients to pay the bills online.

This example makes another point, which is that technology is always evolving. That's also what Alan

In the 1960s, many companies used technology such as the electric typewriter and the dictating machine, a device that recorded one's voice to be played back at a later time.

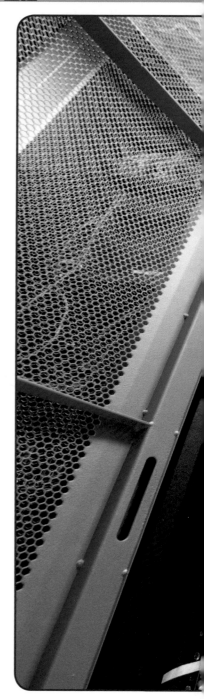

Kay meant in his definition: every generation is introduced to a new era of technology. For ancient people, the invention of paper was technology. It was much better than carving letters into blocks of stone or clay!

A computer program that was used yesterday may be obsolete today. Whenever one company releases a new software or program, other companies rush to offer their own version to compete with it. If you want to work in technology, you may not need a college degree because what you learn in the classroom may be out-of-date by the time you graduate. Because technology is always changing and improving, you may need to have the right personality to work in certain technological fields.

You may be the kind of person who loves to keep up with trends. Maybe you're always playing with new programs or looking for a faster, better way to do just about anything. You may be someone to whom friends turn

The internet is vital to modern business, and computer technicians have the important job of making sure that servers are properly maintained

when they need tech-related help. It could be that technology is your passion, but you're not thrilled about the idea of having to go to college for four years to do something that you love.

This resource will cover a number of jobs that are tech-related for which you don't need a college degree. You will see that in most of them your experience matters more than a diploma. Technology rewards people for what they can actually do, not for what courses they have taken.

According to Alan Kay, technology may mean anything, but here is a list of the tech fields we will cover going forward:

Information sciences and technology: this field works on accessing and processing information for businesses and organizations.

Computer science: this field studies the design and processes of computer-based technology and software.

Computer engineering: this field studies the design and processes of computer hardware.

Marketing: this field focuses on how technology can help companies and organizations market their services and products, either through internet marketing or graphic design.

Communications: this field focuses on how technology helps improve communication, either via text or visuals.

Telecommunications: this field relates to the way in which modern communications (texts, phone calls, broadcasts, emails) are sent over lines and cables.

Social media: this field is defined as the websites and applications (Facebook, LinkedIn, Twitter, and others) that allow people to network and communicate via the internet.

Medical technology: this field involves the creation and crafting of medical devices and appliances, such as eyeglasses, braces, prosthetic limbs, and other items.

In each section, you will learn about a specific career that does not require a college degree. For some positions, you may be able to enter the workforce in an entry-level position and then advance in the company once you have gained more experience and knowledge. While you may not need a college degree for some positions, demonstrating that you have taken some courses post–high school may boost your chances of landing a first job in that field. Some careers may require a certification to begin working or ask you to complete certifications every few years to learn the necessary technology as it is developed and adopted. Some jobs may focus mostly on your portfolio, which is a collection of samples of your best work.

As you read on, you will learn about what someone in that field does and what high school courses you should take to prepare yourself. We will also include a list of resources—books, magazines, and websites—so you can learn more.

CHAPTER 1

SOCIAL MEDIA MANAGER

It seems that everyone today has a Facebook account, but social media has more than just a personal use. Its potential to enhance business opportunities is vast. Companies and organizations use dozens of social media tools (Facebook, Instagram, Reddit, Tumblr, and Pinterest, to name a few) to reach new clients, to test new products, to build marketing campaigns, and for many other purposes.

Therefore, in the past few years a new career has emerged on the scene: the social media manager. Every organization that has a social media presence needs someone to manage its social media traffic.

Most social media managers work 9 a.m.–5 p.m., Monday through Friday, although project deadlines may require them to work evenings and weekends. Here are some of the possible duties of a social media manager:

- Knowing the community or target audience of the company

These company logos, including Facebook, Twitter, Instagram, and YouTube are some of the most widely recognized symbols in the world.

- Using social media to build communities and grow the fan base around the company's goals
- Establishing a reputation for the company online
- Handling budgets related to social media campaigns
- Handling online "traffic"— questions, feedback, and other communications from consumers

How does one become a social media manager? Social media management skills are usually not learned in a college classroom. According to Caitlin Dewey, writing in the *Washington Post*, "Most people currently working in the field picked up their social media skills at home or on the job. The consensus on The *Post's* social media team is that there's no formula for getting a job in this field—we all came from vastly different backgrounds. If there was a formula, however, an academic degree likely wouldn't be part of it."

One of the most important skills a job candidate can have is knowing how social media works and how using it can benefit a particular organization.

Writing in the *Huffington Post*, John Egan agrees with Dewey's assertion: "Many experts in social media don't believe in the power of formal education—through either certificate or degree programs at colleges and universities—for anyone seeking to brush up on social media skills. Conferences, on-your-own learning, and practical experience are better vehicles for absorbing knowledge about social media, they say." One of the reasons is that the social media field is always changing. A program that's widely used today may be irrelevant in a year. Therefore what you learn in a classroom may "expire" by the time you graduate.

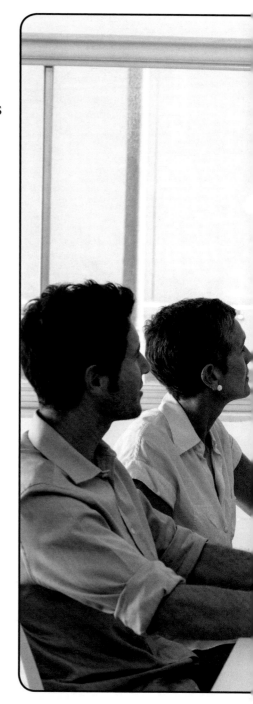

In many fields of technology, being able to communicate your ideas with your clients and coworkers is crucial, but it is not a talent that requires a college degree.

THE SOCIAL MEDIA MANAGER INTERVIEW

When they are being interviewed, people hoping to be hired for a social media manager position can bet on being asked these two questions:

How do you stay up-to-date on the changes in social media? You should be prepared to talk about how you research and experiment with new tools and programs. Give an example of a time when you heard about a new tool and spent a lot of time getting to know it well. Talk about your passion for learning about new, better, faster ways of getting the job done.

How would you improve our company's current social media campaign? Spend some time researching the company's current social media presence. What social media tools is it using now to promote a product or service? How effective is it? How do you know that? In other words, what tools are you using to determine its effectiveness? How could the company make its social media presence even stronger?

PREPARING YOURSELF

Most high schools do not offer stand-alone classes in social media, but many teachers are incorporating social media into their classes. Some teachers have students submit work online and do projects together as online teams. In some classes, students may tweet answers during work sessions, according to a hashtag the teacher has established. While a formal college degree is not needed, some experts advise that you enroll in some online programs or take individual classes. Hootsuite is one site that offers classes on social media, and there are many other affordable online classes or webinars. The best experience is to offer your management services to a company or a friend's business or charity. Do the work, learn as you go, and keep track of all that you are doing so that you can present your experiences to a future employer.

FUTURE PROSPECTS

The Bureau of Labor Statistics (BLS) expects public relations as a field to grow over the next few years. The BLS labels social media managers under the general title of public relations managers or specialists, and it notes in its *Occupational Outlook Handbook* that "public relations specialists are often in charge of monitoring and responding to social media questions and concerns."

FOR MORE INFORMATION

BOOKS

Kawasaki, Guy, and Peg Fitzpatrick. *The Art of Social Media: Power Tips for Power Users*. New York, NY: Portfolio, 2014.

Guy Kawasaki is a pioneer in business marketing and has worked for some of the nation's largest companies, including Apple. In a straightforward, simple manner, he offers over one hundred practical tips and advice for marketing using social media.

Story, Mark. *Starting Your Career as a Social Media Manager*. New York, NY: Allworth Press, 2012.

This book describes the profession of the social media manager and offers tips on how to get your career started in this field. The author is a college professor and a social media professional himself, and his advice is excellent.

Wollan, Robert, Nick Smith, and Catherine Zhou. *The Social Media Management Handbook: Everything You Need to Know to Get Social Media Work in Your Business*. Hoboken, NJ: Wiley, 2011.

This handbook is a thorough, insightful guide to how to work with social media in your business or company.

The handbook is especially useful because it offers advice about how social media managers can work with other departments in a company, such as information technology (IT), sales, customer service, and legal.

ORGANIZATIONS

The Communications Media Management Association (CMMA)
140 Island Way, Suite 316
Clearwater Beach, FL 33767
(561) 477-8100
Website: http://www.cmma.org
The CMMA is over seventy years old, and its mission is to provide professional development and training, as well as networking opportunities for its members, through an annual conference, publications, and regional meetings.

The Social Media Managers Association (SMMA)
Selsey, Chichester
West Sussex, England
Website: http://www.socialmediamanagersassociation .com

The SMMA is devoted to helping its members become more knowledgeable about the field of social media management and find ways to attract new clients while maintaining firm control of their business.

PERIODICALS

Social Media Marketing Magazine (SMMM)
18939 Waterway Road
Dallas, TX 75287
Website: http://www.smmmagazine.com
Social Media Marketing Magazine provides social media tips and strategies for social media managers.

BLOGS

Ignite Social Media
http://www.ignitesocialmedia.com/blog
Ignite Social Media offers daily tips and tricks for using social media effectively, including articles about new research in the field.

Social Media Marketing
http://www.socialmediamarketing.com/blog
The Social Media Marketing blog provides updates on trends in social media and links to resources.

WEBSITES

Due to the changing nature of internet links, Rosen Publishing has developed an online list of Web sites related to the subject of this book. This site is updated regularly. Please use this link to access this list:

http://www.rosenlinks.com/CCWC/tech

CHAPTER 2

MOBILE APP DEVELOPER

The use of applications on telephones and electronic devices (mobile apps) caught on quickly and is pervasive. There are apps for everything from paying your bills to losing weight to getting directions—even applying for a job. Most companies and institutions know that they must develop an app in order to be relevant.

Some apps have long-term use, such as apps designed by a credit card company to help customers pay their bills online. Other apps are designed to be more short-term: for example, a conference may develop an app to help conference attendees

There are apps to help with all aspects of life, including those that allow users to improve their health by tracking their workouts and progress toward a weight-loss goal.

A MOBILE JOB?

If you're a mobile app developer, where do you work? Most mobile app developers work in an office (often surrounded by fellow computer software engineers and developers), but it is possible to work at home, on a train, while traveling—you can be as mobile as your future app. As long as you have access to your development software and can communicate with your employer, you can be almost anywhere.

Here's what you can expect, however: You will be sitting in front of a computer screen for long periods of time. Your hours will usually be regular work hours, but when you are approaching the "launch" deadline for a mobile app (when it will be released to the world), you will probably be working evenings and weekends to make sure to meet that deadline. You can also expect some frustration in this job because your app will be tested at several points in its development, which may require going back to the original design and modifying it many times before a final product is approved.

navigate their way between meetings and events during those few days. Other apps help users keep track of their workouts, grow their gardens more effectively, manage their schedules, or do their holiday shopping.

A mobile app developer is essentially a computer software engineer. As with many careers in technology and especially with mobile app development, the name of the game is not "What is your degree?" but "How good is your app?" In that sense, what you can do means more than what is on your résumé. A company that has seen, and possibly used, your mobile apps may be more willing to hire you to develop apps for them.

On the other hand, you may be able to make an excellent income simply by designing your own apps as a freelance developer. You can earn money from the sales of the apps in many ways.

Many apps sell for a small amount, including as low as under a dollar, but others sell for higher amounts, such as ten dollars or more per download. This alone can generate significant income, but if a mobile app becomes popular, you can also earn money from advertisements. Admob and iAds are two ad networks that will pay you to put banner ads in your apps when they see that your app is being downloaded frequently. For this reason, many mobile app developers will make an app free to download, which increases the number of downloads.

Free apps can generate income in other ways. Other developers will offer two versions of their app: a free app, and then a paid, more developed version. Referred to as "freemiums," the free app will get the user interested

in paying for a more enhanced version, or the "premium" version, of the app. Furthermore, some apps may be free to download, but they require in-app purchases, or items within the app that can only be unlocked with a paid purchase.

Most mobile app developers work 9 a.m.–5 p.m., Monday through Friday, although project deadlines may require them to work evenings and weekends. If you are a freelance developer, you may work according to a schedule set by your preferences and your workload. Some of the duties of a mobile app developer include:

- Creating mobile applications to meet your company's needs
- Writing the program for the mobile app and testing it to make sure it works
- After the app is released, handling changes needed when problems or glitches arise or are detected by users

The creation of mobile apps represents one of the most exciting developments in technology. MoFirst Solutions, a company in India, employs thousands of app developers and programmers.

American high schools may not offer classes in mobile app development, but you may be able to take courses in computer programming, an important knowledge base.

- Working with others to understand what is needed and how a mobile app will fulfill those needs
- Accepting feedback from others in the company who are asking you to develop the mobile app
- Providing documentation for how the program should work
- Updating and modifying the app based upon new demands or requirements

PREPARING YOURSELF

There may be few to no courses offered in your high school that deal specifically with mobile app development, but be sure to take as many computer courses as you can, especially if your high school offers courses in computer software. If you want to become an app developer, a knowledge of computer software is an important foundation to have. You should also take any advanced math classes and any business courses that your high school offers.

According to Sam Laird writing on Mashable.com "[What is] the best way of all to prove you can build something great? Build something great!" Therefore, investigate and "play" with programs like Apple's iOS developer and Intel's App Up Developer Program to begin designing and developing your own apps. Think of solutions that your app offers: What will it help the user to do? Hire a babysitter? Organize their home? Count their calories?

FUTURE PROSPECTS

The field of software development is expected to grow faster than many other fields in the next few years according to the Bureau of Labor Statistics. According to its *Occupational Outlook Handbook,* the demand for application software developers will go up as the need for new applications increases.

FOR MORE INFORMATION

BOOKS

Iversen, Jakob, and Michael Eierman. *Learning Mobile App Development: A Hands-on Guide to Building Apps with iOS and Android*. Boston, MA: Addison-Wesley, 2014.
A helpful guide for those starting out in the field who are trying to learn the basics of mobile app development. This guide is written in language that is easy to understand, and it provides useful graphics and illustrations.

Monefa, Neo. *APPS: The Ultimate Beginners Guide for App Programming and Development*. Paramount, CA: Paramount Publishing, 2014.
No experience necessary! This guide will help you understand how apps work and how to program and build them yourself.

Mureta, Chad. *App Empire: Make Money, Have a Life, and Let Technology Work for You*. Hoboken, NJ: Wiley, 2012.
Mureta's book teaches you how to build mobile apps and market them to the public.

ORGANIZATIONS

ACT: The App Association
1401 K St NW
Suite 501
Washington, DC 20005
(202) 331-2130
Website: http://actonline.org
ACT represents more than 5,000 app companies and information technology firms in the mobile economy. It works to insure that innovators and creative developers are recognized for their work.

Application Developers Alliance (ADA)
1015 7th St NW
Washington, DC 20001
Website: http://www.appdevelopersalliance.org
According to its website, the ADA works to support a global network of developers as "creators, innovators, and entrepreneurs." It promotes the growth of the industry and advocates for its membership on matters of public policy.

BLOGS

Apptology
http://apptology.com/blog
A blog that discusses trends in the mobile app industry
  and offers tips and other resources for developers.

Envatotuts+
http://code.tutsplus.com
A blog that offers tutorials on coding, design, and
  programming apps.

WEBSITES

Due to the changing nature of internet links, Rosen
Publishing has developed an online list of Web sites
related to the subject of this book. This site is updated
regularly. Please use this link to access this list:

http://www.rosenlinks.com/CCWC/tech

CHAPTER 3

TECHNICAL WRITER

Are you the kind of person who not only loves to use technology but also to talk about it? Do people tell you that you have a great way of explaining difficult technological concepts in an easy-to-understand manner? Are you good at expressing yourself? If so, you may have the potential and the talent to be a technical writer.

Technology is being developed every day, but it wouldn't be helpful or useful to anyone if it were not explained carefully. A technical writer's job is to make communication between the customer or user and the company clear and easy.

Most technical writers work 9 a.m.–5 p.m., Monday through Friday, although project deadlines may require them to work evenings and weekends. Most companies that offer a

Technical writers, who must be skilled at both technology and writing, produce customer support manuals, as well as other resource material, for many different organizations.

product or service employ technical writers to do several important tasks, including:

Writing the content for customer support guides and manuals, which are documents that help people use the product or service. These documents help customers get started, solve problems, and understand the scope of what the product or service offers. These guides and manuals may be print or web documents and frequently will be in both formats. They may be a list of Frequently Asked Questions (FAQs) on a website or a manual that is the length of a book.

Providing documentation for company employees who are building the product or developing the service.

Writing the content for other documents that a company or institution may need. For example, some employers may need you to write what are known as white papers. White papers are documents that provide a clear explanation of a technical topic and are often used as marketing tools in the tech industry.

Providing technical editing services. You may be called upon to proofread and edit the documents produced within the company. You may even be asked to fact-check those documents.

Working with developers and specialists to better understand the product or service about which you are writing.

It should come as no surprise that a person who aspires to be a technical writer should have excellent

WRITING MATTERS

Many people have degrees in technical writing. Some may even have a master's degree. However, don't feel that you are at a disadvantage. That diploma doesn't mean much if the graduate has never written or produced her work professionally.

The truth is that writing matters more than anything. You must, as a job-seeker who does not have a college degree, show that you have a passion for writing and technology. You can do this by volunteering your writing services.

Find a project or service a friend or acquaintance is starting up and offer to write the technical documents they need: the manual, technician's guide, frequently asked questions (FAQs), and other necessary texts. You might also attend a technology conference to network with people, offering your services in that way. Even though you are not getting paid, you are building your reputation as a technical writer, so develop these documents carefully, and don't forget to put them in your portfolio. Ask the person for whom you are providing a free service to write you a recommendation letter, commenting on how working with you was a positive experience. Include this in your portfolio as well.

communication skills. You will be explaining concepts that are often complex in a way that will be understandable to a general user.

Some technical writers work from home and use teleconferencing and other methods to connect to their coworkers at the office.

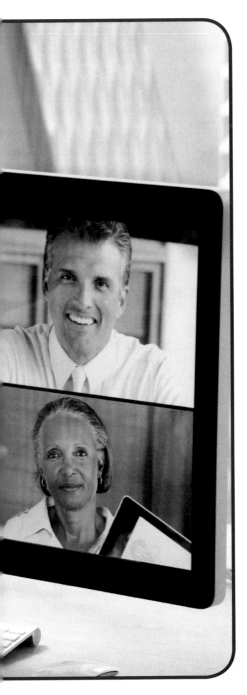

You also need to have a sound foundation in technology because you are the expert who will help the novice user or customer understand every aspect of the product or service. Your area of expertise should line up with the area of the technology industry in which you want to work. For example, if you want to be a technical writer who writes user manuals and guides for social media platforms, you should have a deep understanding of how social media works.

PREPARING YOURSELF

It is important to take as many English and communications courses as your school offers so that you can state on your résumé that you have a strong background in these areas. You might also want to take additional classes in communications and technical writing at a community college or technical school. You will want to demonstrate that you have knowledge of specific technologies, as this is a requirement for many positions in the field. For example, if you are writing a manual for an audio equipment manufacturer, then you will need to show that you have a good sense of how that industry works and what technology it uses.

It is important that you have a portfolio of your technical writing to show potential employers. Writing on the website thewritelife. com, Rob Shimonski advises readers, "Volunteer to help a friend or contact with a project, or create your own. Perhaps you could rewrite support documents for a well-known tool, such as the

Many community colleges offer classes that prepare students to write reports, proposals, guides, and other documents for the technology industry.

iPad how-to manual. Or develop a user guide for a product you enjoy." He also recommends reviewing current products or services in blog posts and other online sites. You could even write sample technical documents to demonstrate your writing skills.

FUTURE PROSPECTS

The job growth rate is expected to be quite high for technical writers, according to the Bureau of Labor Statistics. The Bureau's *Occupational Outlook Handbook* states that "employment growth will be driven by the continuing expansion of scientific and technical products and by growth in Web-based product support."

FOR MORE INFORMATION

BOOKS

Alred, Gerald, Charles T. Brusaw, and Walter E. Oliu. *The Handbook of Technical Writing*. 11th ed. New York, NY: St. Martin's Press, 2015.

Now in its eleventh edition, this handbook is a reliable guide to the field of technical writing. The authors discuss the specific steps to creating a manual, report, or other document. It also includes a handy guide to grammatical errors and commonly misused words.

Morgan, Kieran. *Technical Writing Process: The Simple, Five-Step Guide that Anyone Can Use to Create Technical Documents Such as User Guides, Manuals, and Procedures*. New York, NY: Technical Writing, 2015.

Morgan has provided the ultimate handbook and reference guide for those who want to work as technical writers. It includes useful templates for a wide range of documents that technical writers are required to produce.

Van Laan, Krista. *The Insider's Guide to Technical Writing*. Laguna Hills, CA: XML Press, 2012.

Van Laan offers valuable information about how to write more effective documents and reports. The book also includes a section titled "I Love My Job," which deals with managing the ups and downs of being a technical writer.

ORGANIZATIONS

National Communication Association (NCA)
1765 N Street NW
Washington, DC 20036
(202) 464-4622
Website: http://www.natcom.org
NCA publishes academic journals, organizes workshops
and conferences, and collects data related to the
field of communication, including technical writing
and editing.

Society for Technical Communication (STC)
9401 Lee Highway, Suite 300
Fairfax, VA 22031
(703) 522-4114
Website: http://stc.org
The Society for Technical Communication is one of the
oldest professional associations for people who work
in technical communication, including technical
writers. The STC has members in fifty countries around
the world.

PERIODICALS

Tech Writer Today
http://techwhirl.com
An online resource that offers the latest news about the field of technical communication and content management.

BLOGS

Technical Writing World
http://technicalwritingworld.com/profiles/blog/list
In this blog, users provide reviews of technical communication tools.

WEBSITES

Due to the changing nature of internet links, Rosen Publishing has developed an online list of Web sites related to the subject of this book. This site is updated regularly. Please use this link to access this list:

http://www.rosenlinks.com/CCWC/tech

CHAPTER 4

INTERNET MARKETING

In addition to loving technology, are you good at getting people to listen to you? Maybe you have a critical eye: Do you look at a company's advertisements and feel that it hasn't done a good job in promoting its product? Then you might be terrific at internet marketing, which is the art of getting attention for a product or service.

Companies need marketers to help them generate attention for and interest in their product or service. The competition is fierce, and in recent years much of the marketing has been happening online: in social media, in banner ads, in emails and tweets, in Google search results, and in other forms. The challenge, of

Internet marketing is a highly creative industry, and marketers have to be aware of tthe latest online trends, along with techniques for reaching their audience.

JUST DO IT

Neil Patel, a successful internet marketer, explains in a blog post on quicksprout.com how he learned his profession: "Have you ever heard the saying that you learn by doing? It's actually true. By trying different marketing tactics on your own site, you will learn what works and what doesn't."

As in many other careers related to technology, what you can actually do is far more important that any diploma you can produce. Also, because the internet is constantly changing—five years ago, Twitter was not even imagined to be a possible venue for marketing—there is no university that can offer a degree that would have the most up-to-date skills you need.

A great way to get started is to design and market a website for yourself or a friend, and apply all the strategies you learn from online tools to direct as much traffic as possible to that site. It will be your training ground where you can practice and improve your skills. Don't be discouraged if things don't work out right away. Your goal is to learn and to have something you can put into your portfolio.

course, is that the online audience is huge. Millions of people are online every day and they all have things that distract them, so capturing their interest in the product or service you're promoting is not an easy task.

However, there are strategies and tools that internet marketers use that can be learned fairly easily and that when practiced and applied consistently can advance you in this career.

Most internet marketers work 9 a.m.–5 p.m., Monday through Friday, although project deadlines may require them to work evenings and weekends. Online marketers perform several tasks and jobs for a company, including:

- Assisting the company with its online, email, and social media-based marketing efforts
- Developing a strategy for how to get attention for a product or service through websites, social media, and other tools
- Maintaining a website for the company or its product or service
- Working to generate traffic to a company's website as the number of "hits" a website receives matters!
- Working to make sure that the website places high in a Google search, especially since most users do not go to the second page of a Google search
- Determining ways to generate traffic using mobile apps and smartphones, since many users use the internet on their mobile devices

Many sources have emphasized that marketing requires creativity, and in addition to loving technology, good marketers should have other skills: graphic design skills and

One of an online marketer's jobs is to make sure that a website places high on a Google search to drive traffic to the site.

a talent for writing, programming, and web design, among others. The good news is that you don't need a college degree for these skills either. In fact, one of the most reliable ways to learn some of these skills is to use free online sources such as YouTube videos to help you learn. There are also several Massive Open Online Courses (MOOCs), offered by companies such as Coursera, in which you can take an online course from an expert for free in virtually any topic or subject area.

There are also many tools to keep you aware of changes and developing trends in the marketing industry. These include the online magazines *Search Engine Land* and *Marketing Land. Search Engine Land* covers the field of search marketing and states on its website (www.search-engineland.com) that the magazine provides "breaking stories, industry trends, feature announcements and product changes at popular platforms used by search marketers to reach consumers online." Its sister publication *Marketing Land* features articles written by experts with ideas, tricks, and strategies for running successful online advertising campaigns. Other sites like Moz and Quick-sprout offer posts that can teach you tactics and strategies for online marketing as well.

PREPARING YOURSELF

In high school, make sure to take any writing classes that you can, especially courses in business, technical, and creative writing. You should take any classes offered in computing, web design, and graphic design also. It is important to be skilled in math and data analysis, so make sure you take math classes and know how to read and understand data. You might take classes after high school in graphics, design, and marketing, although you can also do a lot to educate yourself.

You should be aware of courses that are currently promoted online promising that you can become a millionaire by internet marketing, as these are largely scams. Focus on courses offered by companies like Coursera (coursera.org), which are free to enroll in and taught by experts. Try to find a mentor

Taking an online course is an effective way to stay up-to-date about the field of internet marketing, but beware of courses that offer quick money as these are largely scams.

who can guide you through the process and take advantage of all the free reference material available online in videos, blogs, ebooks, and other resources. There may be a wide range of information and ideas online, but with the help of your mentor and other trusted adults, you'll be able to sort through the material to get what you need.

FUTURE PROSPECTS

According to the Bureau of Labor Statistics's *Occupational Outlook Handbook*, the prospect for job growth in the general field of marketing is expected to decline slightly, mostly due to the decline of print advertising. However, the authors of the handbook note that "an increasing amount of advertising is expected to be concentrated in digital media, including online video ads, search engine ads, and other digital ads intended for cell phones or tablet-style computers." Companies will need internet, not print, marketers.

FOR MORE INFORMATION

BOOKS

Baer, Jay. *Youtility: Why Smart Marketing Is About Help Not Hype*. New York, NY: Portfolio, 2013.
This approach to internet marketing advises marketers to be of use to consumers and not just try to grab their attention. Several major companies use this approach and the author describes how to incorporate these methods into the expanding age of internet advertising.

Halligan, Brian. *Inbound Marketing, Revised and Updated: Attract, Engage, and Delight Customers Online*. Hoboken, NJ: Wiley, 2014.
The author describes online consumer behavior that marketers can use to promote their campaigns. It is also a good guide for how to get started in this field.

Scott, David Meerman. *The New Rules of Marketing and PR: How to Use Social Media, Online Video, Mobile Applications, Blogs, News Releases, and Viral Marketing to Reach Buyers Directly*. Hoboken, NJ: Wiley, 2015.
A best-selling guide to marketing using the internet. The author has a step-by-step approach to creating campaigns, writing press releases, using blogs and social media, and other marketing tools.

ORGANIZATIONS

eMarketing Association
40 Blue Ridge Drive
Charlestown, RI 02813
(800) 496-2950
Website: http://emarketingassociation.com
The eMarketing Association provides access to
certifications in online marketing, tutorials, and
other resources. The association has a newsletter for
members to help with networking and online courses
for professional development.

Internet Marketing Association
10 Mar Del Rey
San Clemente, CA 92673
(949) 443-9300
Website: http://imanetwork.org
The Internet Marketing Association is a network of
over one million internet marketers worldwide. Basic
membership is free, and members have access to
podcasts, tips, advice columns, and other information.

PERIODICALS

Marketing Today
7205 Exner Road
Darien, IL 60561
Website: http://www.marketingtoday.com
Published by a marketing consulting company,
   Marketing Today offers internet marketers new
   strategies and techniques for advertising online.

Target Marketing Magazine
9015 Strada Stell Court, Suite 203
   Naples, FL 34109
Website: http://www.targetmarketingmag.com
This collection of blogs and reviews provides tips for
   online advertisers.

WEBSITES

Due to the changing nature of internet links, Rosen
Publishing has developed an online list of Web sites
related to the subject of this book. This site is updated
regularly. Please use this link to access this list:

http://www.rosenlinks.com/CCWC/tech

CHAPTER 5

COMPUTER CODING AND SOFTWARE DEVELOPMENT

A software developer is a person who writes code for a computer program. Software developers write a set of instructions, using symbolic language, to instruct a computer to execute specific tasks or functions. This is also referred to as developing a program or programming.

You might be surprised to know that someone can be a computer software developer without a college degree. Although it is a profession that requires a great deal of skill, there are no specific exams to

Computer coding, which is using symbolic language to tell a computer what to do, is one of the most sought-after skills in the job market.

Dearborn STEM Academy in Boston, Massachusetts, is one of many American high schools that offers computer science classes to its students.

take or credentials to earn to become a developer.

Larry Alton, writing for Business.com, stresses that there is so much demand for these positions that employers cannot fill them quickly enough: "With a growth rate of 22%, these jobs are often unfilled, and employers will often wave your educational qualifications if you know what you're doing."

Writing on the *Guardian's* website, Frank Wales discusses several signs that indicate computer coding and software development may be the right career for you. For example, he says that people who enjoy strategy games like chess and who enjoy problem solving are suited for this profession. Enjoying music and winning arguments are more indicators. Another indicator? A love of technology. "If you want to work in software engineering," Wales states, "you need to have an appreciation for the amazing possibilities that technology brings to the world."

SHOW YOUR PASSION

Software development requires a lot of time spent on computers, immersed in coding. This requires patience and steadfastness, and employers are more likely to hire you if they sense that you actually enjoy this kind of work. As James Burt, writing at guardian.com, explains, "When interviewing candidates for a job, the most important thing many hiring managers look for is enthusiasm. It's not uncommon to interview someone who is qualified for the job but doesn't seem to actually enjoy working with computers."

Do you have this passion? Do you enjoy sitting and working through a problem until the puzzle has been solved? Show your passion for working through the issues and for learning all the latest programs and tools that become available.

As Burt says, "Technical knowledge can be picked up if you have the aptitude, but you can't fake enthusiasm."

Coding is an essential part of the job. There are many ways you can learn coding languages such as SQL, Java, Javascript, and Python. You should also learn the platforms that are in demand and which are being used in the industry. Two websites that might be helpful are the Spring (spring.io), a website that contains tutorials on different platforms, and Stack Overflow (stackoverflow.com), a helpful online community.

Most computer coders and software developers work 9 a.m.–5 p.m., Monday through Friday, although project deadlines may require them to work evenings and weekends. Here are some of the duties of a coder and software developer (also referred to as a software engineer):

- Designing and developing software that meets the needs of a client
- Creating flowcharts that guide programmers as they write the software code for the planned program
- Writing computer code to develop the planned program
- Working with a team of other developers and programmers
- Running tests to make sure the software works
- Documenting every step of the process of developing and writing the program

PREPARING YOURSELF

Many computer software developers have stories about learning how to code by getting a computer and putting in hours and hours of practice. They coded until they had mastered the skill. You should take any classes your high school offers in computer science, information science, and advanced mathematics. If your high school offers any courses in computer programming, take those as well. You should also seek out other ways to learn computer programming. There are many courses available online for free.

Coding is a job that requires more than writing code. It requires you to document how you wrote the code so that others may access it.

FUTURE PROSPECTS

According to the Bureau of Labor Statistics, jobs are expected to grow rapidly in this field due to the demand for computer software. This field is expected to grow much faster than many other occupations.

FOR MORE INFORMATION

BOOKS

Abraham, Nikhil. *Coding for Dummies*. Hoboken, NJ:
For Dummies, 2015.
A fun, easy-to-understand guide to writing code
and developing software. The book contains
illustrations and graphics that make the material
even more user-friendly.

Klimczak, Erik. *Design for Software: A Playbook for
Developers*. Hoboken, NJ: Wiley, 2013.
A handbook for creating programs that users love,
with a companion website that includes design
templates. The author also includes several
useful prototypes.

Sonmez, John. *Soft Skills: The Software Developer's Life
Manual*. Greenwich, CT: Manning, 2014.
This book is about how to be happy in your career
as a software developer. The author covers issues
such as being productive, personal finance, and
career satisfaction.

ORGANIZATIONS

Association for Computing Machinery (ACM)
2 Penn Plaza, Suite 701
New York, NY 10121-0701
(800) 342-6626 (US/Canada)
Website: http://www.acm.org
The ACM addresses issues that affect the field of
computers and establishes standards and codes of
ethics for those working in the profession.

Software and Information Industry Association (SIIA)
1090 Vermont Avenue NW, Sixth Floor
Washington, DC 20005-4905
(202) 289-7442
Website: http://www.siia.net
The SIIA is a trade association for software developers
and digital content creators. It promotes the industry
and helps inform its members about tips and trends.

BLOGS

Joel On Software

http://www.joelonsoftware.com

A blog by programmer Joel Spolsky, who offers reviews
of software products and companies.

Steve's Software Development Blog

http://stevepeacocke.blogspot.com

An information technologist gives his take on software
development and provides introductory information
on the field.

WEBSITES

Due to the changing nature of internet links, Rosen
Publishing has developed an online list of Web sites
related to the subject of this book. This site is updated
regularly. Please use this link to access this list:

http://www.rosenlinks.com/CCWC/tech

CHAPTER 6

GRAPHIC DESIGNER

Graphic design is a way of communicating a message through visual images rather than words. Graphic designers work for all types of industries, and they may produce graphics for all sorts of products or venues: billboards, websites, cereal boxes, store windows, video games, or television commercials. The range and opportunities are vast, and it's an ideal job for someone who loves art and design as much as they love technology.

While many graphic designers today are going to a university or to a design school to earn degrees in the field, you still do not need one. As Kimberly Pendergrass writes in a blog post on udemy.com, "A huge number of fantastic

Companies invest a lot of time and money in developing an identity. or brand, that helps consumers feel connected to their product.

THE PORTFOLIO

If you want a job as a graphic designer, you need a portfolio that highlights your creativity and shows your skills by featuring your most accomplished work.

As Kimberly Pendergrass puts it bluntly on udemy.com, "No one cares about your degree when they hire you. They care about your portfolio."

The all-important portfolio! Every graphic designer talks about it. So what exactly is a portfolio?

Simply put, a portfolio is a collection of samples of your work. For people in fine arts or writing careers, it is an important part of demonstrating—along with their résumé—what their skills are. Job seekers looking for graphic design positions will want to collect images they have worked on, websites they have designed, advertisements they have created, and other samples, and put them into a format (such as a book or a binder) that a potential employer can flip through. In fact, because so much graphic design work is digital today, many job seekers carry digital versions of their portfolio on a flash drive or make them accessable through a cloud storage service. Some will even create a website with their work displayed on it or embed QR codes into their print portfolio that will link the employer to their work samples online.

Ideally, a potential employer should be able to peruse your portfolio and not just understand that you are talented but also sense what kind of style you have. Do you work well with traditional images, or are you more experimental and edgy? Is your sense of design quirky and humorous? It goes without saying that you should only include your best work in this portfolio and update it regularly throughout your career.

designers never went to design school, and just learned their trade as they went along, by reading design books, working with more experienced graphic designers, and most importantly—working in the field. Because what you REALLY need to become a good designer is practice, practice, practice."

When a company needs to advertise a message or promote a product, it will often bring a graphic designer onto the project to create a visual design for the brochure, commercial, website, or whatever platform is being used to advertise that product.

As a graphic designer, you will likely specialize in one of several sub-areas. You may be a logo creator, or you may specialize in typography. You may be a creative director and oversee projects, or perhaps you will be an image editor or work specifically with website graphics.

While a lot of graphic design work can be done by hand if someone is an artist, most graphic design work is done on computers, using technological tools to create, enhance, and manipulate images. These tools include an excellent, high-powered computer, as well as programs like the Adobe Creative Suite, which includes Photoshop, Illustrator, and InDesign. A graphic designer should also have access to a good camera for taking and documenting images for use in one's own designs.

Most graphic designers work 9 a.m.–5 p.m., Monday through Friday, although project deadlines may require them to work evenings and weekends. Most designers work for a company, but some work on a freelance basis, charging companies either by project or by the hour. The graphic designer's job includes:

- Using a combination of art and technology to solve problems
- Meeting with clients before developing a design to determine what is needed for the project
- Developing designs using computer tools to communicate messages through visuals
- Working with shapes, color, fonts, and images to create the visual communication required by their client
- Presenting their designs to the client and then reworking the design based on feedback and suggestions

Graphic designers often work in teams to generate ideas, produce samples, and fine-tune an idea to create a design that appeals to the client.

- Acquiring the business skills to work within a specific time frame and budget

PREPARING YOURSELF

In high school, you should take as many courses as possible in art history, website design, and art. Make sure to take any business courses your high school offers because graphic designers need to understand business concepts in order to work successfully within a company to meet budget limits, work within deadlines, and complete project timelines. It is also a good idea to look for internships with companies that use graphic designers so that you may add some professional work to your portfolio. You might also look to online courses such as those offered by Udemy, many of which are free.

Graphic designers are artists at heart, and being skilled at various art forms such as painting will be beneficial to your success.

KAREN HUANG PHOTOGRAPHY   HOME   BIO   PLACES   PORTRAITS   FEATURES

Creating the look of a particular website like the one shown here (www.khuangphoto.com) is just one of the many career paths that a graphic designer can take.

FUTURE PROSPECTS

According to the Bureau of Labor Statistics, growth is expected to remain steady for graphic designers, although graphic designers will face more competition for jobs. In the *Occupational Outlook Handbook*, the BLS also notes that one in five graphic designers is self-employed.

FOR MORE INFORMATION

BOOKS

Airey, David. *Work for Money, Design for Love: Answers to the Most Frequently Asked Questions About Starting and Running a Successful Design Business*. San Francisco, CA: New Riders, 2012.

The author, a successful graphic designer, offers tricks of the trade and advice on ways to start a career in graphic design and keep it moving forward.

Bruck, Eva Doman, and Tad Crawford. *Business and Legal Forms for Graphic Designers*. New York, NY: Allworth, 2013.

This book contains documents that every graphic designer needs, such as sample contracts, design templates, timeline worksheets, and more.

McNeil, Patrick. *The Designer's Web Handbook: What You Need to Know to Create for the Web*. Cincinnati, OH: HOW, 2012.

McNeil teaches you how to create functional and beautiful designs. There is also great information on how to work with design teams, generate ideas, and work within a budget.

ORGANIZATIONS

American Institute of Graphic Arts (AIGA)
AIGA National Design Center
233 Broadway, 17th floor
New York, NY 10279
(212) 807 1990
Website: http://www.aiga.org
AIGA is a community of professionals who advocate
for the design industry. Originally founded as the
American Institute of Graphic Arts, it is now simply
known as AIGA and has 25,000 members across
the country.

Graphic Artists Guild
31 West 34th Street, 8th floor
New York, NY 10001
(212) 791-3400
Website: https://www.graphicartistsguild.org
Founded in 1995, the Graphic Artists Guild works to
provide professional development and support for
graphic designers. The organization helps promote
their members' careers and artistic endeavors.

PERIODICALS

HOW Magazine
PO Box 421751

Palm Coast, FL 32142

http://www.howdesign.com

This award-winning magazine and website offers reviews of web design products and tools. HOW also sponsors design competitions.

BLOGS

Behance

https://www.behance.net

This blog allows designers to post their portfolios, highlighting their best work.

Dribble

https://dribbble.com

This networking site allows web designers to post their work and share ideas.

WEBSITES

Due to the changing nature of internet links, Rosen Publishing has developed an online list of Web sites related to the subject of this book. This site is updated regularly. Please use this link to access this list:

http://www.rosenlinks.com/CCWC/tech

CHAPTER 7

WEB DEVELOPER

Everyone loves surfing the web looking for entertainment, information, or socializing opportunities. Every page you land on has been carefully designed by a web developer, who also manages the site. Some websites are so intricate that their creators are referred to as web architects.

A web developer is not the same as a web designer, although a developer may perform the tasks of a designer. A web designer concentrates on the look of the website, while a developer makes the website work and determines how people are using the site to access information.

It might surprise you to know that you don't need a college degree to become a web developer. You need a computer, some web design tools, and a lot of practice.

News   Sport   Weather   iPlayer   TV   ~~Radio~~

More Sport ∨

~~T~~IS

~~C~~ricket | Rugby U | Rugby L | Tennis | Golf | Athletics

Draws   Order of Play   Men's Rankings   Women's Rankings

Headlines

Tsonga stuns Federer in quarters 💬 174

Williams fights back to reach semis

Djokovic digs deep to reach quarters

Sharapova into French Open quarters

Federer survives scare in Paris

Serena books place in Paris quarters

Robredo makes history at French Open

Djokovic thrashes Dimitrov in Paris

Haas beats Isner in epic match

~~rapova fights back after losing~~
~~n their quarter-final.~~

French Open: Order of play at Roland Garros

How to follow tennis on the BBC this summer

Live coverage

🔊 French Open
Coverage from Roland Garros Wed 5 June, BBC Sport website

🔊 French Open
Women's singles final, Sat 8 June, 14:00 BST, BBC Radio 5 live

🔊 French Open
Men's singles final, Sun 9 June, 14:00 BST, BBC Radio 5 live

BBC SPORT

BBC RADIO 5 live

BBC RADIO 5 live

French Open Scores & Results

~~les | Results~~

Possessing the skills to develop a website like this one for the BBC (http://www.bbc.co.uk) will make you a valuable member of any organization looking to grow its web presence.

TUE 12:30 PM

Web developers work to make sure a website is available on computers, tablets, and smartphones because consumers like to stay connected wherever they go.

PAY ATTENTION TO DETAILS

Web developers who are successful at their careers often have unique personalities: they are typically people who are curious and always want to try new tools, new programs, and new formats. They are also very obsessed with detail.

They have to be.

As a field, web development ... well, develops every day. New tools and languages are being created daily, and web developers have to try them out and determine if they are going to be useful or not.

Web developers are also hard-wired to be detail-oriented because they know that one small mistake—one mistype or click—can prevent a website from being a success. Web developers are meticulous in their work, and they review and test until they know the project is perfect. They also know that a website is never actually finished and will always require tweaking and updating, and they welcome the chance to continually make it better.

Most web developers work as part of a group that includes designers and programmers to produce a website that meets the specific needs of the client.

As the field grows, however, some people may find it easier to land a job when they have a degree from a college or a university in hand.

However, it is still possible to either land a job based on samples of your work (that is, websites you have created) or get an entry-level job and work your way up through a company based on your work. The bottom line: your career possibilities depend on what you can do!

Most web developers work 9 a.m.–5 p.m., Monday through Friday, although project deadlines may require them to work evenings and weekends. You will likely work for a company, working on in-house projects and sites, but you might also work on a freelance basis.

So, what are the job requirements for a web developer?

- Building a website based on client's needs and requirements
- Using computer coding and web design languages to create a website
- Maintaining and updating the site regularly
- Taking responsibility for getting the site back online in the case of glitches or crashes
- Managing data related to how users are accessing and clicking through the website
- Ensuring that the website is accessible and easy to use
- Creating content for a website, including text and visuals

- Working with illustrators, designers, and writers to make sure project requirements are met

PREPARING YOURSELF

To prepare for becoming a web developer, take any classes your high school might offer in computer programming and website design. Also make sure to take any classes that are available in statistics, business, and writing. As a web developer, you will need to know basic HTML, as well as more powerful scripting languages like JavaScript, and PHP (Hypertext Preprocessor), as well as popular frameworks like jQuery and Bootstrap. You might also look to online courses such as those offered by Udemy, many of which are free, or at Coursera, which are all free. Many developers are fans of w3Schools.com, which offers free tutorials that are easy to access and use.

FUTURE PROSPECTS

The job prospects for web developers are excellent, according to the Bureau of Labor Statistics, and they are expected to grow at a faster rate than the average for all occupations. The high demand for developers is linked to the increasing popularity of e-commerce and mobile devices.

FOR MORE INFORMATION

BOOKS

Beaird, Jason, and James George. *The Principles of Beautiful Web Design*. Australia: SitePoint, 2014.
This book assumes you know how to build a basic website. Its purpose is to teach you how to make your websites pop! There are several chapters that focus on design, color, typography, and other elements of beautiful website designs.

Karlins, David, and Doug Sahlin. *Building Websites All-in-One for Dummies*. Hoboken, NJ: Wiley 2012.
An easy-to-understand guide to web design, with a sense of humor. The book includes helpful graphics and illustrations.

Robbins, Jennifer Neiderst. *Learning Web Design: A Beginner's Guide to HTML, CSS, JavaScript, and Web Graphics*. Sebastopol, CA: O'Reilly, 2012.
This is a terrific handbook for people just starting out with web development and design. The author includes helpful tips for building sites and creating designs from start to finish.

ORGANIZATIONS

International Web Association (IWA)
119 E. Union Street, Suite #A
Pasadena, CA 91103
(626) 449-3709
Website: http://support.iwanet.org
An organization with many chapters across the world, the IWA fosters opportunities for advancement in the web design and web development fields.

WebProfessionals.org
The World Organization of Webmasters
PO Box 584
Washington, IL 61571-0584
(916) 989-2933
Website: http://webprofessional.org
This professional association advocates for the web design and development industry and provides career networking for its members.

PERIODICALS

Net Magazine
Future Publishing Limited
Quay House
The Ambury
Bath, England
BA1 1UA
http://www.creativebloq.com/net-magazine
An online magazine that features reviews and updates
   on internet design and illustration.

WEBSITES

Due to the changing nature of internet links, Rosen
Publishing has developed an online list of Web sites
related to the subject of this book. This site is updated
regularly. Please use this link to access this list:

http://www.rosenlinks.com/CCWC/tech

CHAPTER 8

TELECOMMUNICATIONS TECHNICIAN

The world is more connected today than ever before. Telecommunications are communications—telephone calls (landlines and cell phones), emails, texts, broadcasting, and the like—that occur over a distance via modems, routers, cables, wires, and other means. Technicians are needed both to install those systems and to keep them running and in good condition, so that they can carry increasing amounts of communication traffic. While this field is becoming more and more sophisticated, the career of a

This technician is shown at work wiring telephone equipment. Keeping people connected in our complex world requires telecommunications technicians skilled an installing, maintaining, and reparing telecommunications systems.

Many telecommunications technicians must be able to work wherever the communications equipment may be, including on roofs, in trenches, and on top of telephone poles.

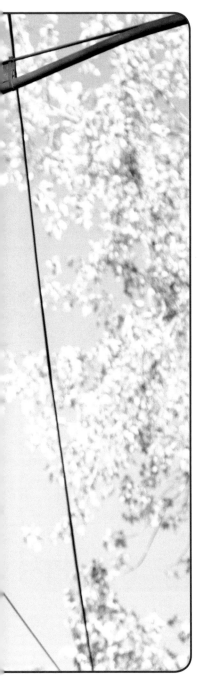

telecommunications technician is one that does not require a college degree.

Most technicians work 9 a.m.–5 p.m., Monday through Friday, although you may have on-call for weekend or evening duties. There may be emergencies, such as blackouts or equipment failures that require flexibility in your schedule. Here are some of the duties of a telecommunications technician:

- Installing, repairing, and maintaining telecommunications systems or equipment
- Traveling to homes and businesses or working within an office environment to perform installations, repairs, and inspections of telecommunications equipment
- Inspecting equipment or systems for problems and implementing fixes
- Testing equipment or systems to ensure proper functioning

SOCIAL SKILLS

A telecommunications technician has to be a people person. Not only must you know how to lay cable lines, climb a telephone pole to inspect a wire, and install a high-speed internet router, but you must also teach your clients how to use the equipment.

Imagine you have been called to a client's home to install a new telephone line. You must have the social skills to make sure the client feels comfortable having you work in his or her home for a significant period of time. Furthermore, once you have completed all the work, you now become the teacher: you must instruct the client on how to access, use, and troubleshoot their new system.

Keep in mind that many of your clients may have very basic information and knowledge of how to use the equipment. They just need it to work easily and with little effort. You must present your information in an easy-to-understand manner and answer any questions thoroughly.

A telecommunications technician is a great career for those who love technology, but it helps if you like working with the public as well.

- Working with cable reels, stripping tools, and trenching machines
- Responding to emergency calls when communications have been interrupted
- Following diagrams to understand and solve problems
- Repairing and installing cabling underground, under floors, or on rooftops or telephone poles

Telecommunications technicians should be able to differentiate between colors to be able to understand wire color-coding. They should also be very good at working with their hands. Technicians should be able to physically work on aerial repairs and underground jobs. You may have to climb a roof or go down into a manhole or a trench to reach cables and wires.

This is a job that requires good problem-solving skills. You may, for example, be called upon to install new cable lines in a very challenging space and you will have to find a solution to the problem. You may be called to a customer's home because their internet has stopped working and they have no idea why.

As a telecommunications technician, you need to diagnose the problem and fix it, usually within a limited amount of time. Customers don't want to hear that they will be unable to use the internet for several days—they usually want it fixed right away. Your job will be not only

Part of the job of a telecommunications technician is being able to determine the problem and repair it quickly so customers can continue working or enjoying their leisure time.

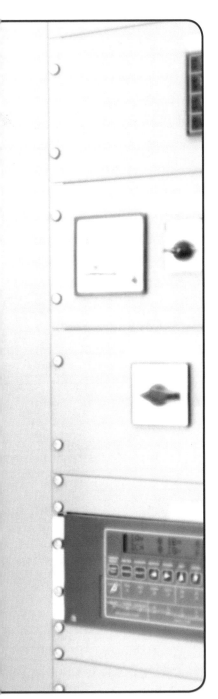

to diagnose and assess the problem but also to provide a reasonable estimation of how long it will take to perform the repairs.

PREPARING YOURSELF

To become a telecommunications technician, it would be useful to take classes in electronics in high school. Classes in computers and communications would also be useful because you'll need a basic level of knowledge in these areas. It may also be helpful to earn a certificate in a program for telecommunications technicians. Some employers will require a license or specific certification, which are often earned through the Telecommunications Industry Association (TIA) or the Society of Cable Telecommunications Engineers (SCTE).

FUTURE PROSPECTS

The demand for this job will decline slightly over the next few years because more people require wireless services, which don't require installation, and equipment is sturdier than ever, requiring less repair. However, job opportunities will open up as companies seek to replace workers who leave the industry. Employees who have strong customer service skills will have the best prospects for landing a job.

FOR MORE INFORMATION

BOOKS

Dodd, Annabel Z. *The Essential Guide to Telecommunications*. New York, NY: Prentice Hall, 2012.
Dodd explains how the telecommunications industry is growing and changing. She also incorporates information about new trends, such as cloud computing.

Newton, Harry. *Newton's Telecom Dictionary*. New York, NY: Harry Newton, 2016.
This dictionary contains more than 27,000 words and phrases used in the telecommunications industry. Easy to use and helpful!

Shepard, Steven. *Telecommunications Crash Course*. 3rd ed. New York, NY: McGraw-Hill, 2014.
Now in its third edition, Shepard's book covers the way in which IT infrastructure, the mobile device environment, and broadband transport depend on each other.

ORGANIZATIONS

National Cable and Telecommunications Association (NCTA)

25 Massachusetts Avenue NW, Suite 100

Washington, DC 20001

(202) 222-2300

Email: webmaster@ncta.com

Website: https://www.ncta.com

The NCTA is an association that works with the
television and internet industries to advocate for
public policy that supports those fields.

The National Coalition for Telecommunication
Education and Learning (NACTEL)

Website: http://www.nactel.org

This is a premier institution for education
and certification opportunities in the
telecommunications industry.

Telecommunications Industry Association (TIA)

1320 North Courthouse Road, Suite 200

Arlington, VA 22201

(703) 907-7700

Website: http://www.tiaonline.org

Founded in 1924, the TIA works on the development
of telecommunications industry standards, business

opportunities, and events for its members to network and advance their careers.

PERIODICALS

Telecom Engine
Telecommunications Media Group
  685 Canton Street
  Norwood, MA 02062
(781) 619-1969
Website: http://www.telecomengine.com
Telecom Engine is an online source of
  telecommunications news and industry trends.

WEBSITES

Due to the changing nature of internet links, Rosen Publishing has developed an online list of Web sites related to the subject of this book. This site is updated regularly. Please use this link to access this list:

http://www.rosenlinks.com/CCWC/tech

CHAPTER 9

COMPUTER SUPPORT SPECIALIST

Most work tasks performed today have been moved onto computer platforms. When you receive a delivery, for example, you will often sign for it on a computer. At your grocery store, the cash registers are really computers that scan, tally, and total your purchases. Companies automatically assign their employees a computer to help them perform their jobs efficiently. Computers help employees perform their duties in American offices, schools, and institutions—until they stop working.

That's when a computer support specialist is called. A computer support specialist may work with the general public, via telephone, chat, or email, or in a company as part of a team to support

Many computer support specialists work in call centers, such as this one in India, where they provide support for clients via computer and telephone.

company employees. A computer specialist's job is to help people address and resolve any computer-related problems they are having as quickly as possible. In some companies, these employees may also be referred to as help-desk technicians.

The computer support specialist may walk a customer through the computer problem over the phone, or he or she may come to an office or home to figure out the issue.

To be good at this job, you have to, of course, really like working with computers and know how they work. According to the Bureau of Labor Statistics, to be a computer support specialist you need to be knowledgeable about computers, but you don't necessarily need a college degree. Taking a few computer courses may be enough. Some employers may require an associate's degree or certificates beyond high school, or you may gain an entry-level position in a company and advance within the company by earning certificates.

Most computer support specialists work 9 a.m.–5 p.m., Monday through Friday, although customer support hours may require them to work evenings and weekends. You may work in a call center or in an office for a company. Some computer support specialists may be able to work from home and set their own hours.

Computer support specialists spent most of their time communicating with clients and helping them resolve their technology problems as quickly as possible.

THE INTERVIEW

If you're interviewing for a position as a computer support specialist, you can expect a few specific questions:

You will most likely be asked why you want to work in this field. You should emphasize not only your passion for computers but also the fact that you like to work with people and help them solve computer-related problems.

You might be asked what you are looking for in a new position, or what types of challenges you are expecting. Your reply should stress that you enjoy challenges and that you are looking forward to expanding your skills and continually learning.

You might also be asked why you want to work at a particular company. This is always an interesting question because the interviewer is trying to determine whether you are a good fit for the company. This is your opportunity to prove that you have done your research about the company (hopefully, you have!). Talk about the fact that you have always wanted to work in the specific industry in which the company specializes, whether its focus is in telecommunications, video game development, nonprofit work, or another field. Try to link past experiences you may have had with the company's goals.

A computer support specialist may be responsible for the following tasks:

- Troubleshooting problems, such as program glitches, computer crashes, and software issues
- Working efficiently and communicating clearly and reassuringly with customers who are experiencing computer problems

It is important to receive regular training in new computer technology and trends so you are able to help your clients resolve their technological problems.

- Training customers or company employees on new technology and software updates
- Handling multiple calls or requests at a time and being able to prioritize which problems should be handled first
- Providing reports and documentation about service hours and management
- Staying current on new technology updates and programs
- Advising the company or customer about new technology purchases and investments

PREPARING YOURSELF

To prepare for a career as a computer support specialist, enroll in any high school courses that are available in computer science and information technology. It may also be useful to take a communications or public speaking class. Take advantage of any classes offered in any kind of specific computer programs, like Microsoft, Cisco products, and others. Advanced math courses will also be helpful to add to your knowledge base.

FUTURE PROSPECTS

According to the Bureau of Labor Statistics, the need for computer support specialists is expected to grow in the next several years as organizations continue to upgrade their equipment and software.

FOR MORE INFORMATION

BOOKS

Beisse, Fred. *A Guide to Computer User Support for Help Desk and Support Specialists*. 6th ed. Boston, MA: Cengage, 2012.
This complete handbook for help-desk techs and computer support specialists contains useful information on how to troubleshoot problems, offer excellent customer service, train computer users, as well as other tips.

Gibson, Darril. *Effective Help Desk Specialist Skills*. Indianapolis, IN: Pearson IT Certification, 2015.
This book covers the "soft skills" (personal skills) and the "hard skills" (technical knowledge) you need to be an effective computer support specialist. It includes author's notes and additional sidebar information to explain concepts in more depth.

National Learning Corporation. *Personal Computer Support Specialist Trainee*. Syosset, NY: Passbooks, 2014.
This is a study guide for certification tests that computer support specialists may need to take during their training.

ORGANIZATIONS

Computing Technology Industry Association (CompTIA)
3500 Lacey Road, Suite 100
Downers Grove, IL 60515
(630) 678-8300
Website: http://www.comptia.org
With more than 2,000 members, CompTIA describes
itself on its website as "a leading voice for the
technology ecosystem." CompTIA works with
companies across the technology industry to
provide opportunities for IT training and professional
development, and also serves to advocate for
its members.

Customer Service and Support Professionals (The CSSP)
High Tech High Touch Solutions, Inc.
14241 NE Woodinville-Duvall Road
PMB 426
Woodinville, WA 98072-8564
(425) 398-9292
Website: http://www.thecssp.com
A community established for computer support
specialists and help desk technicians, the CSSP
provides its members with networking events and
opportunities for training and development.

BLOGS

HelpDesk.com
http://www.helpdesk.com/welcome-to-the-
  helpdeskcom-blog
This blog offers a great number of resources for help
  desk employees, including job listings, reports on the
  industry, and more.

WEBSITES

Due to the changing nature of internet links, Rosen
Publishing has developed an online list of Web sites
related to the subject of this book. This site is updated
regularly. Please use this link to access this list:

http://www.rosenlinks.com/CCWC/tech

CHAPTER 10

MEDICAL APPLIANCE TECHNICIAN

A medical appliance technician creates, repairs, and modifies medical, dental, and ophthalmic devices such as eyeglasses, braces, prosthetics, hearing aids, and other products. He or she uses various types of material (plastic, leather, metal, among others) to create a range of medical devices. Patients who require these devices have been affected by an accident, disease, an amputation, a birth defect, or by aging. This is an important field, as medical appliances are being developed every day to improve the lives of patients.

Medical appliance technicians usually work in a laboratory or office setting, 9-5, Monday through Friday. They may be hired by companies that manufacture or produce the appliances or devices. They might also work in a health care setting, such as a hospital or health care clinic. Their duties may include:

- Creating medical appliances or devices according to specific work orders and prescriptions

A dental lab technician works in a laboratory to create a set of dentures for a patient. Medical appliance technicians are professionals who help people improve their quality of life.

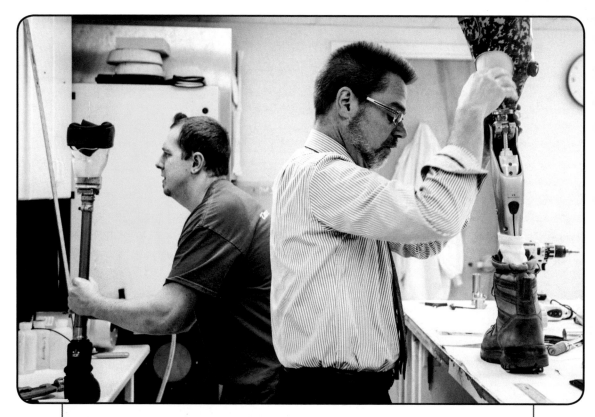

Medical technicians help create and adjust prosthetic devices for their clients. The technician shown here is working on creating a Triton ankle for a patient.

- Shaping and manipulating materials used in forming the appliances and devices
- Using machines and power tools to create or repair devices
- Repairing and maintaining appliances and devices
- Working with doctors, patients, and other team members to insure the best fit for the patient

THE POWER OF PROSTHESES

One of the most exciting advances in modern medicine is the development of devices that allow disabled people to participate in activities that once seemed impossible.

A prosthesis (the plural form is prostheses) is a medical device that replaces a missing body part, such as an arm, leg, hand, or even a missing joint. Missing teeth can be replaced with dental prostheses, and even specific bones, such as a jawbone, can be replaced with a device. These types of prostheses can liberate disabled people and empower them to go beyond the limits of what they thought they could do. For example, a person who had to experience a leg amputation may be able to run a marathon as a result of their prosthetic legs.

A medical appliance technician's role is to make a cast of a body part for which a patient requires a prosthesis. Then the technician uses that cast, as well as digital scans of the patient's body, to make the prosthesis out of plastic, resin, or another material. The technician will use tools to carve, shape, cut, and weld the prosthesis to fit the needs of the patient. The ability to make these devices is a remarkable skill to have and one that has a direct benefit to the lives of others.

Medical appliance technicians should enjoy working with their hands, as they will have to operate machinery and handle medical appliances. They also have to be detail- oriented and

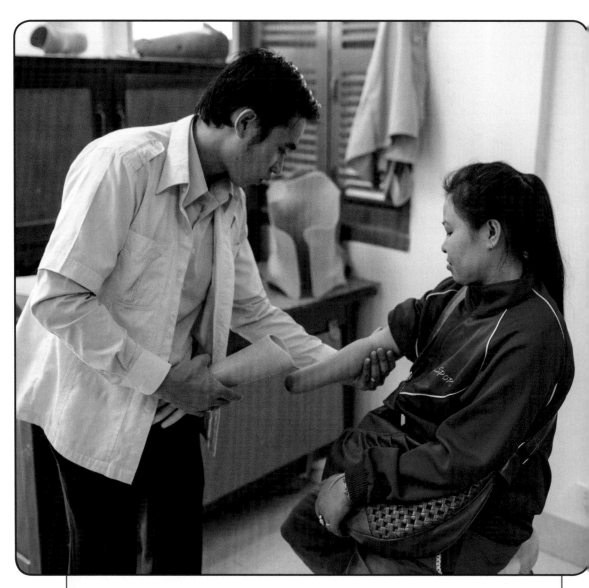

A medical techician helps a woman in Laos with her prosthetic arm. There are may victims of landmines and cluster bombs in Laos who need such appliances.

willing to keep working on a project until it is completed successfully. Medical appliance technicians should be able to read instructions and prescriptions precisely and accurately.

A high school diploma is all that is required for this position. Most medical appliance technicians receive their training on the job, starting out as assistants in a lab and working their way up as they gain skills and experience. Some certifications are available for this career path through the National Commission on Orthotic and Prosthetic Education (www.ncope.org).

PREPARING YOURSELF

In its *Occupational Outlook Handbook*, the Bureau of Labor Statistics recommends that high school students who want to work as a medical appliance technician take classes in math, science, computer programming, and art. Learning how to use and operate a variety of machinery and computer programs is also helpful.

FUTURE PROSPECTS

According to the Bureau of Labor Statistics, the demand for medical appliance technicians is expected to grow over the next several years as more Americans have a need for medical devices and appliances.

FOR MORE INFORMATION

BOOKS

Johnson, Tony, David Patrick, Christopher Stokes, David Wildgood, and Duncan Wood. *Basics of Dental Technology: A Step by Step Approach.* 2nd ed. Hoboken, NJ: Wiley-Blackwell, 2016.
This introduction to dental prostheses includes helpful illustrations and charts.

Netter, Frank H. *Atlas of Human Anatomy: Including Student Consult Interactive Ancillaries and Guides.* 6th ed. New York, NY: Saunders, 2014.
Written by a respected medical doctor, *The Atlas of Human Anatomy* is a colorful and helpful guide that is used widely in the health and medical fields. It is a useful reference book that you will keep throughout your career.

Stanfield, Peggy. *Essential Medical Terminology.* Burlington, MA: Jones and Bartlett, 2015.
This dictionary of medical terms and language is indispensable for anyone working in the medical field.

ORGANIZATIONS

Medical Equipment & Technology Association (META)
http://www.mymeta.org
Medical Equipment & Technology Association (META)
  is an organization for professionals that service
  and support equipment in the health care industry.
  META has the mission of being the focal point
  for resources, networking, and activities that will
  promote growth and unity for all in this profession.

National Commission on Orthotic and Prosthetic
  Education (NCOPE)
330 John Carlyle Street, Suite 200
Alexandria, VA 22314
(703) 836-7114
info@ncope.org
Website: http://www.ncope.org
According to its website, NCOPE "promotes education
  in the field of orthotics and prosthetics and raises the
  standards of education in the field."

PERIODICALS

Biomedical Instrumentation and Technology
4301 N. Fairfax Drive
Suite 301
Arlington, VA 22203
(703) 525-4890
Website: http://www.aami.org/publications/BIT
BI&T magazine features in-depth articles for people in
the profession, as well as updates on new technology
and other developments in the field.

WEBSITES

Due to the changing nature of internet links, Rosen
Publishing has developed an online list of Web sites
related to the subject of this book. This site is updated
regularly. Please use this link to access this list:

http://www.rosenlinks.com/CCWC/tech

GLOSSARY

APP The short term for "application," or a computer program used for a specific purpose.

CALL CENTER An office used to make or accept phone calls, often to sell a product or service.

CERTIFICATION A specialized test someone must pass to be able to work in a particular field.

CODE The set of instructions, written in symbols, that are used in a computer program.

CUSTOMER SERVICE The process by which a person handles the requests, questions, and complaints of a customer.

DOCUMENTATION Written instructions about a project or program that helps others understand how it works.

FREELANCE The condition of working for oneself rather than for a company. Freelancers have set rates and charge either by the project or by the hour.

HARDWARE The physical equipment used in the field of technology, such as a computer or other machine.

HELP DESK The division of a company where customers or employees can get help with their technology needs.

INNOVATOR Person who brings fresh ideas to the development of a product or service.

MARKETING The advertising or promoting of a product or service with the aim of selling that product or service to a customer.

MEDICAL APPLIANCE A device such as braces or a prosthesis that supports a patient's health and mobility.

METICULOUS Paying close attention to each detail of a project.

MOBILE Related to technology that is portable, such as cell phones or tablets.

PORTFOLIO A collection of one's best work, or samples of one's creative output.

PROGRAM A set of instructions that a computer can understand and perform.

RÉSUMÉ A document listing a person's qualifications for a particular job.

SOFTWARE The programs used in technology and computing.

TECHNOLOGY The application of science to industries such as business, medicine, and other fields.

TELECOMMUNICATIONS A network of routers, cables, and lines upon which communication traffic moves (including phone calls, text messages, and internet communications).

BIBLIOGRAPHY

Alton, Larry. "Seven Tech Jobs You Can Get Without a Degree." Business.com. May 20, 2015 (http://www.business.com/technology/7-tech-jobs-you-can-get-without-a-degree).

Bureau of Labor Statistics. *Occupational Outlook Handbook*. December 17, 2015 (www.bls.gov/ooh).

Burt, James. "How to Become a Software Developer Without a Degree." The *Guardian*. November 3, 2014 (http://www.theguardian.com/careers/careers-blog/how-to-become-a-software-developer).

Dewey, Caitlin. "Here's How to Get a Job in Social Media Without Spending $27,000 for a Master's Degree." *Washington Post*. September 18, 2013 (https://www.washingtonpost.com/news/the-switch/wp/2013/09/18/heres-how-to-get-a-job-in-social-media-without-spending-27000-for-a-masters-degree).

Egan, John. "Do You Need a Degree in Social Media?: No Way, Some Experts Say." *Huffington Post*. July 29, 2014 (http://www.huffingtonpost.com/john-egan/do-you-need-a-degree-in-s_b_5630531.html).

Greelish, David "An Interview with Computing Pioneer Alan Kay." *Time Magazine.* April 2, 2013 (http://techland.time.com/2013/04/02/an-interview-with-computing-pioneer-alan-kay).

Laird, Sam. "So You Want to Be a Mobile App Developer? Here's How." Mashable.com. August 27, 2012 (http://mashable.com/2012/08/28/app-developer-infographic/#b5oOcd20Eaqd).

Louie, Kaitlin. "How to Become a Technical Writer." Schools.com. April 28, 2014 (http://www.schools.com/articles/career-toolbox-technical-writing.html).

Patel, Neil. "How I Learned Online Marketing (And How You Can Too)." Quicksprout.com. December 16, 2013 (https://www.quicksprout.com/ 2013/12/16/how-i-learned-online-marketing-and-how-you-can-too).

Pendergrass, Kimberly. "What Does a Graphic Designer Do? The Industry Revealed." Udemy.com. February 27, 2014 (https://blog.udemy.com/what-does-a-graphic-designer-do-2).

Shimonski, Rob. "Want to Be a Technical Writer?" The Write Life. December 23, 2014 (http://thewritelife.com/how-to-become-a-technical-writer).

Wales, Frank. "10 Signs a Career in Coding and Software Development Might Be for You." *Guardian*. January 24, 2014 (http://www.theguardian.com/careers/ten-signs-career-coding-software-development-right-for-you).

Young, Nikki. "Tips to Becoming a Successful Internet Marketer." ClickBank.com (http://www.clickbank.com/tips-to-becoming-a- successful-internet-marketer).

WEBSITES

Due to the changing nature of internet links, Rosen Publishing has developed an online list of Web sites related to the subject of this book. This site is updated regularly. Please use this link to access this list:

http://www.rosenlinks.com/CCWC/tech

INDEX

ABOUT THE AUTHOR

Susan Nichols lives and works in Baltimore, Maryland, where she teaches writing. Learning tech skills has become an important part of teaching and writing, so Nichols has been developing online classes using Twitter and Facebook to create learning communities, as well as conducting most of her research using internet tools.

PHOTO CREDITS: